I've Done Some Really Dangerous Things With Hula Hoops
by Skip Wood

All rights reserved. Printed in the United States of America.
No part of this book may be used or reproduced in any written form or by
electronic or mechanical means, including information storage and
retrieval systems without written permission from the author, except
for the use of brief quotations in a book review.

Illustrations/Interior Design/Book Cover by: Joe Figueroa - Figzart.com

Copyright ©2020 by Skip Wood

Paperback ISBN: 978-1-953806-14-7
Hardcover ISBN: 978-1-953806-15-4
EBook ISBN: 978-1-953806-16-1

Published by: Spotlight Publishing - https://SpotlightPublishing.Pro - Becky Norwood

Quotations and Smiles by Skip Wood

INTRODUCTION

In 2014, I had taken a much-needed break from education after being a high school Physical Education teacher for 16 years. After a year away, I weighed my options and decided it was best to return to teaching. The new PE position I accepted, however, required me to teach a couple of classes at an Elementary school, something I had never done. I had no idea what I was getting into!

I was teaching High School PE in the morning and Elementary PE in the afternoon and as you might expect, there's a vast difference between the two settings. It's a constant battle getting high school students to put forth effort, or even participate, during PE class. That is not the case with Elementary kids! Elementary classes enter the gym like a tornado and the storm doesn't end for 30 minutes. It can be overwhelming and frustrating at times, but it's always an adventure and their energy is contagious. I made it a goal to always try to match the kids' enthusiasm and in turn, it rekindled my fire to teach.

The things Elementary kids say during class are entertaining, to say the least, and quickly became my favorite part of the job. I realized early on that if I asked a question about the day's activity, the chance of the answer having anything to do with it were slim to none. Early on in my return to teaching, I remember asking a Kindergarten class if they had any questions about the "Jump Rope for Heart" video we had just watched to kick-off a school fundraiser. Everyone's hands immediately shot up and I decided to call on a girl that looked like she was going to burst if she didn't get to answer. She loudly and proudly exclaimed, "My family is getting new carpet in our house tomorrow!"

From that point on I knew I should write down some of these interactions and share them.

Enjoy!

This book is dedicated to my son Rex, who inspires me everyday.

1st grader #2: "Mr. Woody, guess how I broke my foot!"

Me: "Playing soccer?"

1st grader #2: "I put my mom's high heels on and jumped off a dresser!"

Me: "That was totally my next guess."

Me: "You've fallen down 3 times already and we've only been in class for 5 minutes."

1st grader: "When I get tired, it's all over Mrs. Woody."

Me: "It's Mr. Wood."

Me: "That's the rules of the game, any questions?"

Kindergartener #1: "I just want you to know that I've never played this game, but I already love it!"

Me: "Awesome. Any other questions?"

Kindergartener #2: "I can tell you're chewing gum, but you're my favorite teacher so I won't tell anyone ok?"

Me: "Thanks buddy. Any questions about the game?"

Me: "Those are the rules to the warm-up activity. Remember, before I ask if there's any questions, your question has to actually be about the activity ok? So, any questions?"

Kindergartener: "We learned about weather today. It's not snow storms that blow houses down, it's blizzards."

Me: "Alrighty. Let's get started."

1st grader: "Mrs. Wood?"
Me: "It's Mr. Wood, but yes?"
1st grader: "That kid over there is bothering me."
Me: "I'll talk to him, but 'that kid over there' is your twin brother so YOU may want to get used to it."

Me: "How's your day going young lady?"

Kindergartener: "Well, I found a booger on my backpack this morning. Other than that fine."

1st grader: "Mr. Woody?"

Me: "It's Mr. Wood, but yes?"

1st grader: "Do you want me to tell you everything I know about Goblin sharks?"

Me: "Can it wait until after class?"

1st grader: "It really can't."

1st grader: "May I use the bathroom?"
Me: "You may go when your classmate gets back. You know the rule, one student at a time in the..."
1st grader: "I'm already kind of going."
Me: "Hustle."

First Grader: "We got a new puppy, her name is merlot."

Me: "Merlot?"

First grader: "My mom said that is her favorite kind of soda!"

Me: "Why are you crying?"

Kindergartener: "The ball hit me and broke my leg a little bit."

Me: "It's a beach ball."

Kindergartener: "That's why it's not completely broken."

Me: "Questions on the activity?"

Kindergartener #1: "My mom saw you on the computer and she said you have 6 abs!"

Me: "That's not a question."

Kindergartener #2: "My brother's fish had a baby last night!"

Me: "Also not a question."

Kindergartener #3: "I have 2 controllers now if you want to come over and play me in Minecraft!"

Me: "So no questions then?"

Kindergartener: Can I talk to you Mrs. Wood?"
Me: "Um, Sure."
Kindergartener: "It's Serious: I have to whisper it to You."
Me: "Oh."
Kindergartener: I know you said it doesn't matter who the fastest kid in class is, but It's me isn't it?"

Kindergartener: "Mr. Wood?"

Me: "You got my name correct! How may I help you?"

Kindergartener: "That kid over there almost kicked me in the leg."

Me: "I will almost tell him to not do that ok?"

Kindergartener: "Thanks Mrs. Wood."

ABOUT THE AUTHOR

Skip Wood is an Arizona-based, South Dakota-raised entrepreneur and fitness enthusiast. Skip looks back fondly on his 19-year physical education teaching career, particularly the final 3 years spent in the Elementary setting. Skip left the teaching profession to start a gym (AZFITCO) and sports supplement company (Muscle with a Motor) with his wife Amanda. Skip loves helping others reach their fitness goals and is able to use both businesses to do so.

Skip and Amanda enjoy an active lifestyle with their three teenage kids in Gilbert, AZ. Their favorite activities include mountain biking and paddleboarding.

The End

www.ingramcontent.com/pod-product-compliance
Lightning Source LLC
Chambersburg PA
CBHW041232240426
43673CB00010B/312